A TRUE BOOK™

The Most Endangered
Big Cats

KATIE MARSICO

Children's Press®
An Imprint of Scholastic Inc.

Content Consultant
Dr. Stephen S. Ditchkoff
Professor of Wildlife Sciences
Auburn University, Auburn, Alabama

Library of Congress Cataloging-in-Publication Data
Names: Marsico, Katie, 1980–
Title: Big cats / by Katie Marsico.
Description: New York, NY : Scholastic, Children's Press, 2017. | Series: A true book | Includes
   bibliographical references and index.
Identifiers: LCCN 2016028988| ISBN 9780531227268 (library binding) | ISBN 9780531232774 (pbk.)
Subjects: LCSH: Felidae—Juvenile literature.
Classification: LCC QL737.C23 M2749 2017 | DDC 599.75—dc23
LC record available at https://lccn.loc.gov/2016028988

© 2017 Scholastic Inc.
All rights reserved. Published in 2017 by Children's Press, an imprint of Scholastic Inc.
Printed in China 62
SCHOLASTIC, CHILDREN'S PRESS, A TRUE BOOK™, and associated logos are trademarks and/or
registered trademarks of Scholastic Inc.
1 2 3 4 5 6 7 8 9 10 R 26 25 24 23 22 21 20 19 18 17

Front cover: A young leopard in Zambia
Back cover: A lion mother and cub

Find the Truth!

Everything you are about to read is true *except* for one of the sentences on this page.

Which one is **TRUE**?

T or F Hunters only kill big cats for their fur.

T or F Tigers and snow leopards are endangered.

Find the answers in this book.

Contents

THE BIG TRUTH!

Already Extinct

19th century
illustration
of a tiger

A lion near
Nairobi, Kenya

A vet holding
a tiger cub

Uporny the tiger climbs out of a vehicle as he's released into the wild.

CHAPTER 1

A Wild Rescue

In May 2015, **conservationists** enjoyed a rare and rewarding sight in the Russian Far East. After months of caring for an Amur tiger named Uporny, they released him back into the wild. The big cat had just spent time in a wildlife **rehabilitation** center before his return to the wilderness. In November 2014, wildlife officials had captured Uporny because he had been identified as a "conflict" tiger.

 No two tigers have the exact same pattern of stripes!

People may be hurt if tigers or other big cats venture into populated areas.

Struggling to Survive

Three-year-old Uporny is called a conflict tiger because of concerns that he would attack humans. A lack of wild **prey** had made the young tiger hungry and desperate. Uporny had been venturing close to areas where people lived and was attacking their dogs. Conservationists worried that the big cat's behavior would lead to serious problems with local residents. Fortunately, he was brought to a wildlife rehabilitation center before this happened.

Big-Cat Behaviorists

Want a full-time job watching big cats? For certain scientists, monitoring how these felines behave is the focus of their career. Animal behaviorists evaluate animals' actions and what they mean. Those who work with wild species sometimes use what they learn to rehabilitate big cats. They help decide if, when, and how conflict animals such as Uporny should return to the wild.

A staff member pets a tiger being cared for at a rescue center in Thailand.

At the center, researchers examined Uporny and studied his behavior. After months of close observation, the experts decided he could safely return to the wilderness. They selected a new habitat with higher populations of wild prey. The region was also home to a female tiger, which made it more likely that Uporny would **mate**. By helping Uporny, conservationists supported one of several big cats facing **extinction**.

Animal researchers often focus on studying a certain type of big cat.

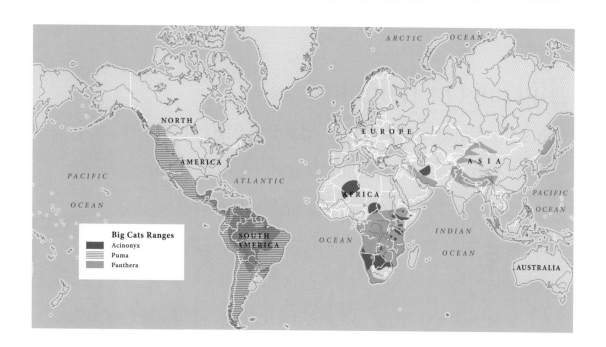

A Brief Overview of Big Cats

Big cats are large, **predatory** cats. These toothy felines are found around the world. They are generally grouped into three different genera, which are categories of related species. Big cat genera include *Panthera* (lions, tigers, jaguars, leopards, and snow leopards), *Acinonyx* (cheetahs), and *Puma* (cougars). All big cats are carnivores, or meat eaters. Most are known for their fierce hunting skills.

Big Cats in Trouble

Despite being powerful predators, big cats face many threats. The wildlife trade, conflicts with humans, and the destruction of natural habitats all represent major problems. Conservationists consider jaguars and leopards near threatened. This means extinction is likely to become a real threat someday. The threat level increases for lions and cheetahs, which are vulnerable. Species in this category face a higher risk than jaguars or leopards, but are not yet considered endangered.

There are an estimated 6,700 cheetahs left in the wild.

A snow leopard can wrap itself in its tail to keep warm.

The risk is even higher for tigers and snow leopards. These cats are endangered, which means they face a very high risk of extinction. Cougars, also known as mountian lions or pumas, are the only big cats that aren't currently at risk. But like many big cats, their survival is in no way guaranteed without the support of conservationists.

Snow leopards are often hunted illegally for their soft, thick fur.

Clouded leopards are excellent climbers.

CHAPTER 2

Fantastic Felines

Most big cats have a physical build that goes hand in hand with their impressive hunting abilities. Their muscular body often allows them to run, leap, climb, and swim. In addition, some have legs that are longer in front than in back. This feature helps big cats such as cheetahs sprint. Cheetahs are Earth's fastest land mammals and are able to reach speeds of 70 miles (113 kilometers) per hour!

Clouded leopards eat everything from pigs to porcupines!

Powerful Predators

Some big cats, like cougars, have extra-long hind legs. This special feature gives them the ability to jump far distances. Cougars can leap 15 feet (4.6 meters) in a single bound! Other big cats excel at climbing or swimming. For example, leopards have been known to carry prey twice their weight up a tree while tigers have no problem swimming between islands in the **mangrove** forests of Bangladesh and India.

A cheetah chases down an impala.

Many Kinds of Cats

Exactly how big are big cats? Size varies among different species and subspecies. Their habitats also cover a range of possibilities.

A COMPARISON OF BIG CAT SPECIES				
Photograph	**Species**	**Weight**	**Range**	**Habitat**
	Cheetah	77 to 143 pounds (35 to 65 kilograms)	Parts of Africa and a small section of Iran	Grasslands, mountains, and some woodlands
	Cougar	75 to 158 pounds (34 to 72 kg)	North America, Central America, and South America	Forests, swamps, and mountains
	Jaguar	100 to 250 pounds (45 to 113 kg)	North America, Central America, and South America	Forests, grasslands, swamps, and mountains
	Leopard	1,320 to 2,090 pounds (599 to 948 kg)	Africa and Asia	Forests and grasslands
	Lion	265 to 500 pounds (120 to 227 kg)	Sub-Saharan Africa and India	Grasslands and forests
	Snow Leopard	77 to 121 pounds (35 to 55 kg)	Central Asia	Mainly higher mountain areas but sometimes forests
	Tiger	220 to 660 pounds (100 to 300 kg)	Asia	Forests, swamps, and grasslands

A snow leopard's spots help it stay hidden. Can you spot the snow leopard in this photo?

The Functions of Fur

Big cats' fur is among their most recognizable features and protects them against weather extremes. It also makes them effective predators. For example, leopards' spots actually help them hunt. Thanks to their coloring, they blend in with their environment as they move across patches of sunlight and shadows. Because of this, leopards are capable of **stalking** prey without being seen.

Super Senses

Big cats don't rely heavily on smell. It's their other senses that give them a deadly edge in the wild. These fierce hunters have night vision so they can track down food in little to no light. Big cats can also detect a wider range of sounds than most humans do. But that's not all. Their facial whiskers help them explore their environment through touch. They help the cats feel their way through the dark.

Whiskers help cats determine the size and shape of objects.

A jaguar cub sits on a log in Brazil.

Wild Weapons

Like most felines, big cats typically have 30 teeth. Incisors are the teeth used for holding and biting. They are located toward the front of the mouth. Carnassials, in the back of the mouth, help big cats cut and slice their food. Two pairs of long, sharp canines surround the incisors. Big cats use these teeth to stab into the flesh of their prey.

Carnassials

Incisors

Canine teeth

Each type of cat tooth serves a particular purpose.

Most big cats have claws that retract, or pull back into their toes, when not in use.

Bladelike claws are another feature that big cats use to hunt and attack. Some of these predators have nails up to 4 inches (10 centimeters) long! They use their claws to grip prey. Depending on species and location, big cats often eat deer, antelope, zebras, buffalo, and wild pigs. Livestock, bears, monkeys, and armadillos are also big-cat prey.

Unlike some other cats, tigers don't mind spending time in water.

Life Span and Living Space

In the wild, the majority of big cats have an average life span of 10 to 20 years. They make their homes in several types of habitats, including forests, grasslands, deserts, swamps, and mountains. Within these settings, some big cats have dens, or hidden lairs. Den sites range from rock piles to caves to thick clumps of bushes. Other big cats prefer to spend time near or in trees.

Solitary or Social?

Most big cats are solitary, or prefer to be alone. Cheetahs are one exception to this rule. Sometimes two to three males form groups known as coalitions. Lions are also social animals. They live in groups called prides. A pride includes anywhere from 2 to 30 young and adult cats. Male lions help protect the group and its **territory**, while females hunt and care for young.

For most big cats, males tend to be larger than females.

A pride of lions usually has up to 10 adults. Cubs can bring the number up to 20 or 30 lions.

Cat Communication

Communication between big cats is far more than roaring and purring. Hissing, growling, moaning, yowling, and chuffing (snorting) are other noises they make. Big cats also show emotions by moving their ears, eyes, mouth, and tail a certain way. They exchange information through scent as well. Smells created by physical waste and bodily odors are used to mark territory and attract mates.

Lions and other big cats use a range of sounds to express their feelings.

Cougar cubs play in the snow.

A Closer Look at Cubs

Big cats usually have one to four cubs in a litter. For cheetahs, however, a litter can have as many as eight babies.

Cubs are born with their eyes closed. At first, they rely on their mothers' milk for nourishment, but she eventually teaches them to hunt prey. It takes a while for big cats to become fully independent. Some remain with their mother for more than two years.

Already Extinct

For some big cats, it's already too late to fight extinction. Read on to learn about big cats that once ruled their wild habitats.

American Lion

Extinct: About 13,000 years ago
Probable cause: Habitat and climate changes

American lions roamed mountain grasslands throughout North America. But it's possible these extinct predators were more closely related to jaguars and tigers than lions. These terrifying hunters were larger than modern lions and had longer, stronger legs.

Bali Tiger

Extinct: No later than early 1950s
Probable cause: Overhunting and habitat loss

Before the 1950s, these big cats had existed on the Indonesian island of Bali for thousands of years. Bali tigers were the smallest tiger subspecies. Most weighed no more than 220 pounds (100 kg).

Zanzibar Leopard

Extinct: As recently as 1996

Probable cause: Overhunting

These big cats once lived on the Tanzanian island of Zanzibar, off Africa's eastern coast. Occasionally, people still claim to glimpse one, though such reports remain unconfirmed.

Barbary Lion

Extinct in the wild: 1920s

Probable cause: Overhunting and disease

These big cats used to be one of the largest subspecies of lion. Barbary lions were primarily found in forest and mountain habitats in northern Africa. Their dark mane flowed over their shoulders and down to their stomach.

A Future at Risk

Threats to big cats pose serious problems not just to the cats themselves, but also to whole **ecosystems**. As apex predators, big cats sit at the top of the food chain. If big-cat populations decrease, the number of animals they hunt, such as zebras, goes up. More animals mean more food, such as plants, will get gobbled up. That means there won't be enough food for other animals. This ripple effect disrupts natural balance.

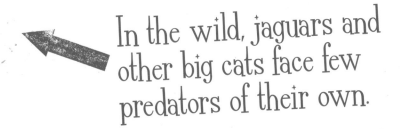

In the wild, jaguars and other big cats face few predators of their own.

Poacher Prey

Big cats are important to their ecosystems. This is why many people are trying to address issues that challenge big-cat survival. The wildlife trade is one major threat. It has driven big cats such as Amur leopards and Amur tigers dangerously close to extinction. Scientists estimate that roughly 60 Amur leopards remain in the wild. Poachers, or illegal hunters, often kill them to sell their fur.

An Amur Tiger Timeline

Mid-1800s

There are roughly 1,000 Amur tigers in the wild.

1940s

The Amur tiger population falls to just 40 cats.

1947

The Soviet government prohibits tiger hunting.

Poachers also kill big cats for their body parts. People buy them as ingredients for traditional medicines. For example, some cultures believe a tiger's bones, teeth, skin, and eyes have special healing qualities. These body parts are frequently ground up and used to treat everything from sleep problems to skin conditions. Such medicines result in the slaughter of more than 100 tigers a year.

May 2015
The Amur tiger Uporny is released back into the wild.

2015
There are as many as 540 wild Amur tigers.

A lion rests near Nairobi, Kenya. The nearby city skyline is a reminder of how the habitats of humans and big cats often overlap.

In some cases, hunters shoot big cats during trophy hunts. This type of hunt is intended to prove a person's skill at hunting.

Human-animal conflicts can also lead to big-cat deaths. When big cats wander onto farms or near villages, they often spark tension and fear. People kill them in hopes of preventing attacks on livestock, pets, and human beings.

Lion Lights

In 2011, Richard Turere was walking around his family's farm in Kenya with a flashlight. The 11-year-old noticed that nearby lions seemed afraid of the motion of the light. Inspired, Richard hung LED bulbs on farm posts. He wired these bulbs to flicker. This made it seem like the lights were moving. Richard's "lion lights" now successfully prevent attacks on livestock. This further reduces conflict between farmers and big cats.

Nowhere To Live

Big cats tend to venture outside their wild habitats because they are losing living space. People cut down trees for timber and other products. They clear grasslands and drain swamps to construct farms, roads, and buildings. These activities have a disastrous impact on the natural areas where big cats hunt and **reproduce**. Many have already disappeared from much of their original range.

Big Cat Populations

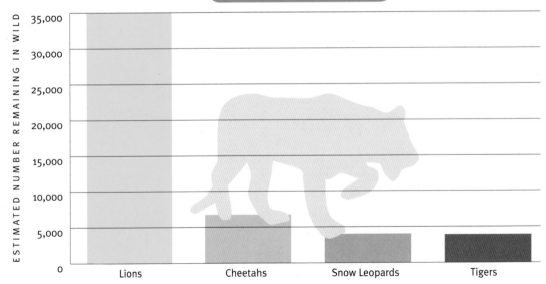

ESTIMATED NUMBER REMAINING IN WILD

35,000
30,000
25,000
20,000
15,000
10,000
5,000
0

Lions   Cheetahs   Snow Leopards   Tigers

SPECIES

Some experts predict the snow leopard's range will shrink more than 20 percent by 2050 due to climate and other changes.

Feeling the Heat

Many scientists argue that global warming is also taking a toll on big-cat populations. Pollution adds harmful chemicals to the atmosphere. This causes Earth's temperatures to increase. Ocean levels rise and coastlines erode, or wear away. Droughts, or extremely dry spells, become more common. The ice in snowier regions melts. These changes threaten the places that big cats make their home—and the resources they need to survive.

A vet holds a
recently rescued
tiger cub in
Germany.

CHAPTER 4

A Chance to Change the Story

Many big-cat populations are in serious trouble, but conservationists still have hope. Some conservation efforts focus on creating and enforcing stricter antipoaching laws. Other people work to establish protected areas such as national parks. In these places, human changes to natural habitats are restricted. Conservationists also aid big cats that are injured or are conflict animals. They care for these felines in **sanctuaries** and rehabilitation centers.

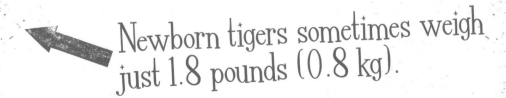

Newborn tigers sometimes weigh just 1.8 pounds (0.8 kg).

Getting the Word Out

Education is a huge part of big-cat conservation. Efforts to teach people more about these incredible creatures and the threats they face take many forms. Scientific research programs, presentations at schools and zoos, and television commercials are just a few. Conservationists help people find new ways to live peacefully alongside wildlife.

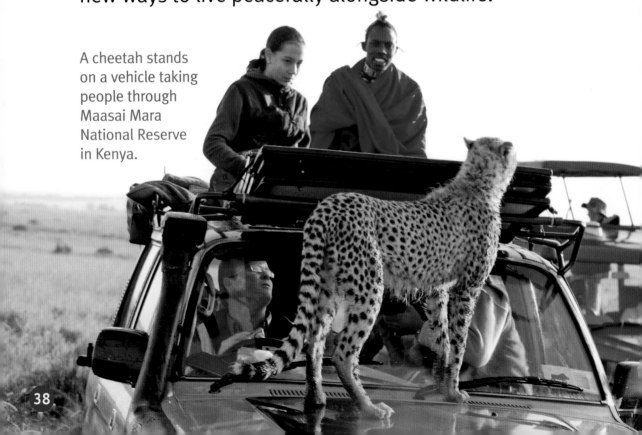

A cheetah stands on a vehicle taking people through Maasai Mara National Reserve in Kenya.

Big Cat Comeback

Conservation efforts are beginning to pay off. In 2016, four countries confirmed that their tiger populations are growing. That year, experts estimated there were 3,890 tigers in the wild. Just six years before, there were as few as 3,200. It was the first time in a century that tiger populations showed any growth.

There is still a long way to go. Tiger and many other big cat numbers remain dangerously low. Still, conservationists are working hard to help these animals roar back before it's too late! ★

A tiger cub snuggles up to its mom.

CALLING ALL CONSERVATIONISTS!

Conservationists represent all walks of life. Some are scientists. Others are kids just like you! What can you do to help? Here are a few ideas to get you started:

CELEBRATE!

International Tiger Day is on July 29! Visit tigers at the zoo with your family and friends. Or make a list of steps you can take to help preserve tiger habitats. For example, pollution and global warming are likely destroying natural areas where tigers live. To fight pollution, walk and bike instead of driving!

VISIT A SANCTUARY

Go online with a trusted adult to learn the location of the one nearest you. Find out if this facility allows visitors. If it does, plan a trip there. If it doesn't allow visitors, ask staff or volunteers for more information about their work.

CREATE A CAMOUFLAGE COLLAGE

Big cats' fur provides them with camouflage, or the ability to blend in with their surroundings. Search for pictures of big cats in magazines. Cut out images of their fur and paste them to poster board. Or if you prefer, use crayons and markers to draw the different patterns you notice. Your collage should be filled with spots, stripes, and a variety of colors! Share your collage with others to teach them about these amazing animals.

"ADOPT" A BIG CAT

For a small fee or donation, zoos and rescues sometimes allow people to "adopt" animals. Don't worry—you won't be inviting a lion or leopard into your home! But your money will help fund a big cat's care. In addition, you'll probably receive photos and updates related to your adoptee.

Should Big Cats Be Kept as Pets?

Today, many laws restrict the ownership of wild animals. Owners who keep big cats argue that doing so is neither dangerous nor cruel. People who oppose the practice say it is unsafe, unkind, and impractical.

Which side do you agree with? Why?

Yes People should be allowed to keep big cats as pets!

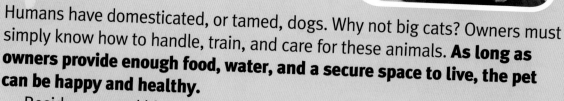

Humans have domesticated, or tamed, dogs. Why not big cats? Owners must simply know how to handle, train, and care for these animals. **As long as owners provide enough food, water, and a secure space to live, the pet can be happy and healthy.**

Besides, several big cats face countless threats in the wild. **Keeping them as pets is keeping them safe.** Big cats that were the victim of trafficking are sometimes not healthy enough to return to the wild. These animals need a place where they can receive care and protection. And if big cats mate in captivity, perhaps their young could be introduced into the wild.

Finally, big cats provide pet owners with learning experiences. **It's both exciting and challenging to care for a wild animal as it grows and changes.** Many people come to view big cats as family members, not fierce predators.

No People should not be allowed to keep big cats as pets!

In many states, it is illegal to own big cats, and for good reason. **Removing big cats from the wild makes them dependent on humans for survival.** That can cause problems for populations already facing extinction, especially since some wild species rarely successfully mate in captivity.

It's also very expensive to take care of big cats. As cubs, they are cute and cuddly. But as they get bigger, these natural-born hunters need a lot of meat to eat and space to roam. When it proves too difficult for owners to meet these needs, **wild pets are often abandoned or abused, or they end up dead**.

Keeping big cats as pets is risky too. **It's almost impossible to completely tame these powerful predators.** Since 1990, authorities in 44 U.S. states have reported more than 300 dangerous incidents involving big cats. In many cases, the cats were being kept as pets. Sometimes, both humans and animals lost their lives. For everyone's sake, it's better to keep big cats in the wild.

True Statistics

The weight range of most big cats: 66 to 660 lb. (30 to 300 kg)

The running speed cheetahs are able to reach: 70 mph (113 kph)

The distance cougars are capable of leaping: 15 ft. (4.6 m)

The number of teeth big cats typically have: 30

The length some big-cat claws reach: 4 in. (10 cm)

The average life span for the majority of big cats (in the wild): 10 to 20 years

The number of cats in a lion pride: 2 to 30

The average size of most big-cat litters: 1 to 4 cubs

How many Amur leopards remain in the wild: Roughly 60

How many tigers are killed each year to make traditional medicine: More than 100

Did you find the truth?

F Hunters only kill big cats for their fur.

T Tigers and snow leopards are endangered.

Resources

Books

De la Bédoyère, Camilla. *The Wild Life of Big Cats*.
New York: Windmill Books, 2015.

Hutchison, Patricia. *Snow Leopards*. Mankato, MN: The Child's
World, 2015.

**Visit this Scholastic Web site for more information
about big cats and to download the Teaching Guide
for this series:**

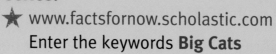 www.factsfornow.scholastic.com
Enter the keywords **Big Cats**

Important Words

conservationists (kahn-sur-VAY-shuhn-ists) people who protect valuable things, especially forests, wildlife, natural resources, or artistic or historic objects

ecosystems (EE-koh-sis-tuhmz) all the living things in particular areas

extinction (ik-STINGKT-shuhn) the permanent disappearance of a living thing

mangrove (MAN-grohv) a tropical tree that grows in swamps or shallow salt water

mate (MAYT) to join with another animal to reproduce

predatory (PRED-uh-tor-ee) living by hunting other animals for food

prey (PRAY) an animal that is hunted by another animal for food

rehabilitation (ree-huh-bil-uh-TAY-shuhn) the process of bringing something back to a normal, healthy condition after illness or injury

reproduce (ree-pruh-DOOS) to produce offspring

sanctuaries (SANGK-choo-er-eez) natural areas where birds or animals are protected from hunters

stalking (STAWK-ing) hunting or tracking in a quiet, secret way

territory (TER-uh-tor-ee) a claimed area of land

Index

Page numbers in **bold** indicate illustrations.

About the Author

Katie Marsico graduated from Northwestern University and worked as an editor in reference publishing before she began writing in 2006. Since that time, she has published more than 200 titles for children and young adults. Ms. Marsico is in awe of all big cats but prefers to admire these majestic animals from afar.